This journal belongs to

____

Mobile : ______________________

Email : ______________________

Great to know...

LANGUAGE

The 12 valid characters in the Hawaiian language are:
a, e, i, o, u, p, k, h, l, m, n, and w.

COMMON PHRASE

1. Hello / Goodbye - Aloha (a-lo-ha)

2. Thank you - Mahalo (mah-hah-loh)

3. You're welcome / No problem - A ole palikir (ah-oh-leh pee-lee-kee-yah)

4. Until we meet again - A hui hou (ah-hoo-wee-ho-oo-uu)

5. How are you? - Howzit? (how-zit)

6. Green sea turtle - Honu (hoe-new)

7. Delicious - Ono (oh-no)

8. Wine - Waina (wy-nah)

9. There you have it! - A 'o ia! (ah-oy-yah)

10. Poke seafood bowl - Poke (poh-keh)

ISLANDS

1. Oahu

2. Maui

3. Hawaii (Big Island)

4. Kauai

5. Molokai

6. Lanai

7. Niihau

To Do / To Go

To Do / To Go

Packing List

CLOTHING

ELECTRONICS / GADGETS

TOILETRIES

IMPORTANT DOCS / MISC

expense Tracker

Date	Category	Description	Amount	Balance

expense Tracker

Date	Category	Description	Amount	Balance

expense Tracker

Date	Category	Description	Amount	Balance

expense Tracker

Date	Category	Description	Amount	Balance

Printed by Libri Plureos GmbH in Hamburg, Germany